In My Own Words

In My Own Words

Glenda Dugar

Rev. date: 08/08/2014

To order additional copies of this book, contact:
Xlibris Corporation
1-888-795-4274
www.Xlibris.com
Orders@Xlibris.com
132388

DEDICATION

To all the men and women who have served
and are currently serving in the U.S. Armed Forces.

July 23, 2013

Ms. Glenda Dugar
Xlibris Publishing LLC
Bloomington, Indiana

Dear Glenda:

Thank you so much for sharing your book with me.

As First Lady, I have no greater honor than working with our
troops and their families. The courage and dedication of service
members like you inspire me each day. I hope you know how much
the President and I value your service to our Nation.

Again, thank you for the book. I wish you all the best.

Sincerely,

Michelle Obama

Contents

CHAPTER ONE

My Childhood Memories

For all who dare to remember details about their early childhood memories or whether you choose to forget those fragments that gradually slip out of reach in your memory, either case, life goes by as fast as a dream. I have no twists or turns in my life story. I'm presenting to you the facts of my life as I remember them. I never before wanted to share what I found to be an extraordinary ride. Many women claim that after they experience childbirth, they have these revelations of their life now being complete and have come to full circle. I feel once I became a grandmother, my life has come into full circle, and I would now like to share my life story with you. I have included photographs throughout my book to help share my experience with you. Picture taking has been a hobby of mine since I was first able to afford a camera in my early teens.

I believe every day is a blessing, a gift from God—my creator—life itself from your first breath. I have a simple way of looking at life—enjoy every day as if it is your last. A common cliché, a well-known phrase, words to live by, often heard, and quoted by many. I remember I realized this at an early time in my life, maybe around the age of six or seven.

I felt I had to take the bull by its horns and just go for it. I realized life would not last forever and people leave this life for many reasons: diseases, accidents, and illnesses that can cause one to have a very short life span. This was a devastating thing to come to grips with as a child. That one powerful thief of life was "CA," the abbreviation for cancer, which takes many lives. Coming to terms with this knowledge as a child was an eye-opening and thought-provoking situation; how debilitating this thing was, and how many lives are taken by this thing alone. It appeared to strike randomly, regardless of how careful or how old or good you are. I remember at that age, I hoped for a cure for it. So I decided to live my life, my gift, to the fullest and every day to try to use it wisely because it is still a blessing from God.

I watched many children grow up seemingly unaware of the fact that if they just use what is available and free to them, focus on some goal even if the home environment is not ideal or what they may have dream it to be, that with hope and prayer and the belief of the power of God in all of us, they can succeed in anything. I believed that if they held on to hope and get through puberty and the essential years of grade school, high school, and even college, anything was possible. That is what I felt; that is what I hoped every child would believe.

I do realize that for some children, it is more difficult to negotiate some of life's obstacles, and one reason for their failure to succeed is lack of parental guidance. I believe parents must know where their children are (for the child's sake) and what they are doing, at all times. Parenting is a full-time supervising job.

Parents must guide their children through life with direct supervision before and after school hours and especially after dark.

While growing up, I saw several children become seriously injured, missing, and killed because their parents didn't supervise them close enough and didn't know they were out "walking on L tracks" or didn't know with whom they were keeping company with. I believe a parent not knowing where their child is after dark is very negligent.

A friend of mine whom I grew up with recently confessed to me that she was raped as a teenager.

During the time we were young friends, she was allowed to sit on her front porch after dark. She was lured by a couple of young men driving around the block, pretending to be looking for a particular street. She told me they saw her sitting on her porch, and they stopped in front of her house. She said they asked her for directions to a particular address; and when she pointed toward the direction they were searching for, they asked her if she could show them, so she got into the car. Yes, you may say that was foolish, but that is exactly why children need close supervision, especially at night. Many parents consider their children sitting on their front porch a safe place, especially if they are within earshot of their children's voices. Most parents tune in closer when they stop hearing the sound of their child; however, things can happen in an instant.

My mom had a full-time job. That job was taking care of me and my brothers and sisters, all eight of us; my dad made sure of that. My mom was a stay-at-home mom for as long as I can remember. We had a hot meal every day. Can you imagine eight children unsupervised and wandering the streets of Chicago even in the '50s, '60s, or '70s?

My dad told us, "Don't let the streetlight catch you out," and those words rang in my ears many nights when I wanted to remain out just a little longer with some children who were allowed to play well into the dark. I realized upon obeying my dad's orders and once inside the house with Mamma, Daddy, and my siblings, I felt safe. I felt that was where I was supposed to be; in fact, I believe that was the safest place for a child.

Growing up, as far back as I can remember, began in LeClaire Courts projects—low-income family housing located off Forty-seventh Street and Cicero Street, just recently torn down in 2011. That was the first home I remember. My dad didn't earn much money; however, as a child, I felt we had enough. I didn't feel as if we lacked anything. I believed we had all we needed, and looking back now, I realized it doesn't take much to please a child. The eight children and my parents were comforting to one another.

I say this because siblings are close support to one another and strengthen one another; especially when my parents were preoccupied with themselves, we were able to keep each other company. Four boys and four girls can be fun: there were lots of pillow fights, and what a combination of personalities blending together.

I was born on the Fourth of July, and I decided for myself at an early age to "be something" in life. Why not? Being born on the Fourth I think was unusual, or people led me to believe so. I began to notice things of beauty around the time I realized life was very short. I recognized things that made me feel calm and serene, like the leaves on trees blowing gently in the wind and stars that twinkled in the night as if they were trying to communicate with everyone on earth. At the age of six or seven, when I saw the sun rise and set, I believed it was the most beautiful thing on God's earth, breathtaking. I remember thinking that if it can do that every day, surely I can do something with my life too, because I knew life was precious. I was beginning to have a sense of self and being a part of everything surrounding me.

As a child, I had not experienced prejudice toward me until I was about the age of seven. I had a school friend whom, for a short period, I walked home from school with. She and I were about the same age. She lived across the almost-always-empty street that separated my projects from her small bungalow home with her family. I remember one day after leaving school, we had walked home and arrived at her house first; and when I stopped at her front door, my friend invited me in. Her mother was just inside the front-room area. She looked at me, and she said to her daughter in front of me, "Don't ever bring that girl here again." My friend and I never walked home together again. She would also hardly look at me and rarely spoke to me when at school. I knew and had witnessed her mother teach her to have prejudice against different people—or at least to me. I realized that there was a serious line that some people drew between other people and chose not to cross it. In this case, and probably many more, negativity was taught and demonstrated by the parent. I remember feeling that it was my friend who was given limitations, and she had to live within the boundaries that her mom had placed on her. I did miss my friend, and I did feel sorry for her mom.

I recall that when JFK was assassinated, it seemed as if the world was in mourning; everyone wept. The black-and-white television showed the funeral procession. I do remember thinking that a good chance for fairness to all was interrupted, halted; then MLK spoke, and I remember maybe we have another chance at something good to happen for everyone. I said this because even as a child, I liked the way both of them spoke, with some kind of wholesome goodness that made you feel good, like the Andy Griffith character (in *Mayberry*), or the feeling you get when you heard the Hellmann's commercial on TV ("When you bring out the Hellmann's, you've brought out the best"), and the strength in watching WGN Frazier Thomas (*Family Classics*)—how it brought the family together. Bozo the Clown always made you smile, if not laugh. Good things and no worries as a child (now knowing that, statistics show that your child acts out what they watch on television). Then MLK was gone; so much anger was in the streets, looting, fires being set at random, shootings and beatings of innocent people and authorities. I knew this was not the way to express the sorrow or confusion that they may have felt, but I begin to realize it was just like my ex-friend's mom; maybe everyone was just acting without thinking of the outcomes of irresponsible behavior. I thought maybe they just felt that this learned behavior is okay, but I felt our country was going down the wrong path.

How can this happen, not twice, but three times within a short time span? Three good men, all with good words being expressed from their mouths, obviously from their souls. JFK, MLK, RFK—their deaths made me realize we had a big problem with confused people about life itself and lack of boundaries. I saw how bad things happen to good people.

I realized then and again life was short and precious. My thought of loss of life was an eye-opening experience at an early age; my uncle, my dad's brother, was the person I felt close to. I remember how he had picked me up into his arms in my home and said words of comfort to me. My parents were standing nearby, and everyone seemed so happy. I was very young, and I remembered he had made me laugh. I felt he was a happy and high-spirited person. He lifted my spirit that day. Later that year, my uncle had an untimely death; and with the way he lifted my spirit, I named my first child in memory of him.

I focused on adjusting to my home environment (since I had to be in by dark); even in the projects, it was comforting. LeClaire Courts was tucked away on a side of town that had a strange security for its dwellers. A kind of *Peyton Place*, where everyone knew everyone, and it was secure for children because of its boundaries: Cicero Street, I-55, and my ex-friend's subdivision. In the summer months, we even left our main front door open, with only the screen door latched; that was until this madman had his way with seven young student nurses, with only one eyewitness, and then all bets were off. It became Fort Knox around our home, and doors were shut and main doors locked tight at night from that point on. A strange sense of innocence of an era was lost, as when the milkman stopped delivering milk and fresh juice to your door.

Aunt Nellie and Glenda

CHAPTER TWO

Common Sense

While in the fifth grade, I concentrated on keeping myself occupied in the evenings by engaging in reading novels and comic books. Our home was not technically equipped like you would find in the average home today. We had only one television, and my dad made sure we had limited access to that—maybe an hour a day of (noncolor) television. There were no tablets or computers, at least not in our home, so I found myself reading a lot. I really enjoyed reading the huge variety of comic books and novels that were donated to our family by a neighbor, and I went through them all. The comic books included everything from *Superman* to *Richie Rich*, *Casper*, *Archie*, and many, many more.

Absorbing myself into reading paid off; when my mom and I attended my fifth-grade open house, my teacher greeted my mom and told her, "You know, Glenda's recent reading score was equivalent to a ninth grader's." I recall my mom looking down at me but not saying a word.

That was news to me at the same time it was to my mom, and I was just hoping that I also had what my mom considered "common sense," which she has always claimed was better than book sense.

My siblings and I would hear my mom speak this phrase to us when it should have been apparent that we did something without thinking of the consequences or asked a question that maybe we could possibly already have the answer to. I realized, in my mom's opinion, having sound judgment, a good show of brotherly love, and good initiative can assist a child or an adult in facilitating the ability to be able to exercise "good common sense" whenever needed.

As life is about the choices you make, one should always practice to make good choices, as each choice adds to your foundation, your life puzzle.

This rationale may sound simple, but I believe if your foundation—your basic principles of how you view life and respect life itself (older adults may say "your upbringing")—as a child is structured, then there is less likely a chance of the world having their way with you which could result in the child or adult becoming a victim of society.

So I can also say that reading, even comic books and short novels, increased my reading and comprehension level, especially with test taking. Many children today have hours of television and video games taking the place of parents' interventions, interactions, and productivity time. Many of the video games are violent and have sexual content. I believe you mimic what you study. That was my first concrete experience with cause and effect. Reading = increased comprehension = good scores = accolades (just like what many studies and research have proven).

CHAPTER THREE

My Singing Debut

We moved to the Austin area in my seventh grade. I went into the seventh grade with a sense of confidence and a feeling that I was beginning to know who I was as a person—about the time of identity versus role confusion as Erikson would predict. The new neighborhood brought new challenges; not only did the neighborhood appear vast, but also the children at my new school seemed less structured than what I was accustomed to. I was beginning to think it was actually going to be a challenge for me to assimilate with them, because it appeared that most of the kids' "upbringing" was more flexible than I was accustomed to being around. It was just a different neighborhood, and many of the students at this new school appeared to be more mentally exhausting for me. I remember one day in class, we all had to take turns giving an oral book report of our choice, and one girl who appeared to be a year older than all of us (possibly just overweight) gave her report on *Sweet Sweetback,* a story about a pimp, of all things. It had sexual content, and she appeared to have no shame in "sharing" this story with the class. The class was uneasy; however, they showed it in giggles, and I remember just sitting there looking at her while she spoke, thinking to myself that not only did the "big" girl have a lack of discretion and judgment issues (no doubt stemming from her home) but also the teacher. I drew the conclusion that the teacher had allowed her to finish her oral report and not interfere so as to not embarrass the girl and possibly affect her self-esteem.

I believe that teacher should have screened the book of each child to ensure that the appropriate information would be presented by everyone. What really bothered me was that I sensed that the girl was getting a kick out of getting away with telling her racy story in class, and she was also letting us know just how she was more sexually advanced than the rest of the class. I was just happy when she sat down.

I felt things in my life were moving right along. I was about to graduate from eighth grade from my new school in my new neighborhood, and I was really looking forward to going into high school. Our teacher made it clear that learning the preamble of the U.S. Constitution among other mandatory requirements that every eighth grader had to know would be tested. I've never forgotten the preamble once I memorized it, and the phrase "to form a more perfect union" to me are the most unforgettable words used in that preamble.

Only weeks from graduation, one of our daily routines as a graduating class was the singing rehearsal of our graduation song, "Climb Every Mountain," from the soundtrack of the musical *The Sound of Music*.

The entire class gathered on stage for each rehearsal. The teacher had this girl sing the chorus, "A dream that will need all the love you can give, every day of your life for as long as you live." After which the rest of the graduating class would join in. Each time the solo singer for the chorus part sang, she would shriek the "for as long as you live" part. After hearing this far too many times and watching the entire graduating class grimace without saying one word to her nor the teacher (as if it sounded okay), I sang out the chorus with her the next time she sang it. The teacher stopped playing the piano and asked, "Who was that?" Because of the crowd, she could not see me, but the kids surrounding me said, "Glenda." The teacher then asked me to sing it again, and we started from the top, and the part was mine.

I knew that the class wanted someone to sing that part better; after all, what was all the practice for if we were going to sound bad at the only eighth-grade graduation we would ever have? I sang that verse as sweet as I could on graduation day, and in the audience my mom just looked.

CHAPTER FOUR

High School Daze

It was very convenient to have my high school located merely several feet from my home. My front door literally faced the school parking lot. My experience of high school was a whole new level of freedom of expression for me. I felt there was less direct supervision my parents had to focus on me, and I seemed to have more opportunities to express my independence, and I had a chance to demonstrate my maturity to my parents and teachers. I knew I needed to choose curriculums that had a combination of things I wanted to learn and I was also familiar with to help keep my grade point average up so I wouldn't have any problem in the future transitioning into the school of my choice. I chose sewing, in which my mom taught me that skill in grade school, and I figured I could make an easy A in that class; and I also chose home economics class. Of course I had the mandatory classes to negotiate along with integrating driver's education toward the end of my freshman year. My oldest sister, Ruthie, helped me with the challenge of learning to drive with her vehicle, and we found the school parking lot very convenient for that purpose. I was meeting new friends, and I chose friends whom

I felt were not only fun to be with but also levelheaded because I didn't want to spend too much energy trying to figure out where they were coming from.

I had one girlfriend who lived on the next block who also attended my high school, and both of us at the end of our freshman year of school decided to try out for one of the sport activities that the school had to offer. I had decided I would not try out for the cheerleaders because I felt they were overrated and far too "loved" by the entire school, and I felt it was partly because of their skimpy and way-too-short skirts. My friend and I decided to give the majorettes a try. I had in the past seen my oldest sister practice with the baton, and I felt somewhat comfortable with it. I had seen the girls on the majorette team in the hallways before, and I felt they had a more sophisticated persona. The captain and cocaptain were twins, and I thought that was special. My friend and I, along with several other girls, tried out for this practically out-of-reach challenge. I created a routine, and after showing it to my sister, she fine-tuned it and said, "Add a cartwheel." And then she gave my girlfriend a few tips also. They chose only two girls that year: me and my friend. I gave thanks to my sister's input, for without that cartwheel that seemed to wow the team judging us, I may not have been selected.

My oldest sister has been a leader for me, and I looked up to her and still do. I expect her to be the one to console me when I'm in doubt and when I'm hurt. While growing up, she has been like a surrogate mother to me, especially when my mom was preoccupied. I would go to my sister for advice or explanations. I feel bad that when I was a child, I took the walnut shell off her swing skirt back in LeClaire Courts. I really believed a nut was inside.

My sister, who is four years older than me, stayed only two years at the high school located across the street from our house. My sister led the way and traveled downtown Chicago to Jones Commercial High School, a business school, for her junior and senior year. I did the same, as my brother Derrick after me and my brother Gregory after him. I rejected becoming the majorettes' captain or cocaptain at the end of my sophomore year as those positions became open because all the current majorettes were graduating seniors. I was still excited to leave all that for Jones Commercial High School because I did see the good things this school was producing.

Many people were aware of Jones Commercial as being an exceptional high school; however, many students chose not to attempt to excel for the challenges this school had to offer. A big factor that many students felt was unappealing was that Jones Commercial had a grade point average requirement for entrance. Also many students became comfortable with their current high school and chose not to leave their current school for one reason or another—sometimes a love interest or just making the move to transfer credits. I believe the main reason why many students refused to transfer to this school was because of its dress code.

I took that chance to change high schools, in hopes it would later prove that I did indeed make a good choice. The opportunity was there. I made the choice, and I believe that the choice I made had good results.

High school majorette

CHAPTER FIVE

Times of Change

During my freshman and sophomore year, my dad appeared to have more discretionary cash. I realized our family was evolving for the better. Our country was going through a commercial growth, and businesses were flourishing; local summer low-pay jobs were available to help the average child ages twelve to seventeen to earn some cash, and day camps and two-week summer camps were becoming increasingly popular. During one neighborhood summer job, an opportunity arose where our supervisor approached our group while we were having a short break out of the sun, and he said, "Who would like to go on an airplane ride, for free?" I could not believe only two of us raised our hands. I thought, how come these kids didn't find this opportunity intriguing? This resulted in only a handful of us traveling on that Delta flight with the president of that airline for my first hour-long flight. As a young teen, I felt that was an experience of a lifetime; again I thought I chose well, and I couldn't understand why the other teens didn't see that as an opportunity to experience something new.

There were several television shows to help depict the black family in those times of upward change and struggle. There were three black family television shows I found interesting and very influencing: *Good Times*, *The Jeffersons*, and *The Cosby Show*. *Good Times* showcased a family that was always just getting by; they never had money for luxury items.

Their food cabinets always appeared bare, and they lived in a high-rise project depicting overcrowding, and there's an elevator that was not expected to be functional 50 percent of each day, and of course they lived on a ridiculously high floor. However, they had love.

The Jeffersons gave you a successful husband with a very supportive wife. He owned a dry cleaner and they also lived in a high rise and had a black maid. However, he was portrayed as self-indulgent, arrogant and conceited, and *always* rude to the maid. He believed he had moved up to a better lifestyle; however, his attitude and behavior reflected that negative behavior was a side effect of his so-called "better" lifestyle.

The Cosby Show highlighted a middle-class family with a husband and wife with professional occupations, "doctors," with a home in a middle-class neighborhood. The father role was portrayed as a family head with personal convictions to have discipline and control of his family and friends of his family by administering the right amount of encouragement and support to his apparently intelligent children—all no doubt were eventually college bound. He allowed his children to exercise their judgment on personal issues they may have been struggling through, thus allowing them to grow and improve their problem-solving skills with less direct supervision from both he and his wife. He appeared to incorporate compassion for his wife and children while using plenty of humor as part of his character.

This family setting was very effective in influencing the television viewers of the possibility of the black family actually succeeding and enjoying life to its fullest. I applauded that show.

I believe family dialogue and family time is very important, and the seemingly more and more old-fashioned concept of having dinner together can reveal much of what is going on with each member of the family.

During this quality family time, parents can analyze how their children's table manners, diction, and health are progressing. I believe this is a good opportunity to provide direction to your family and for the parents to display to them interest in their concerns.

I feel a parent's job of providing discipline to their children is always evolving and requires a constant assessment of how much do you intervene as the child grows. I refer to this as "active parenting" because of the constant changes you must make in your interventions; it is a physical and mental job.

Too much direct intervention can result in not allowing your child to feel free in expressing themselves (unlike the girl giving the book report in my seventh grade, who demonstrated lack of direction), but your goal is to allow your child be free to think outside the box respectfully, thus building their self-esteem. I've found that the combination approach (direct and indirect) to discipline and counseling your child and even adults has a better outcome. I've learned that as your child gets older, less directives and more interjections, as a psychiatrist would do in a conference with you, will lead to better outcomes. This approach will allow a child or even an adult to make their own decisions with you being involved in the supervision of their decision.

In all interventions, how you decide to intervene greatly depends on the child's maturity level and their willingness to cooperate. Therefore, you may have a discipline problem to address before growth begins.

I was very proud of all these television shows that displayed family love and strong attempts to try to understand and get along with one another. Most important, it demonstrated the black family working as a unit, and they were showing Americans that we really were moving on up.

CHAPTER SIX

The Family Vacations

My dad speaks fluent Spanish. I'm proud of that. I know that my oldest sister expressed to me that she wished he had sat down with us (even at the dinner table) and taught his children how to speak the language. I believe that with eight children, my dad was too busy trying to ensure that our English was effective. I was just happy he had the language skill, and for me that meant he was thinking on different levels, and technically his brain had generated many different pathways to accommodate that comprehension and learning. I was also proud of my dad for having this skill, because I knew that for a black man living in the '70s, speaking a second language fluently was special, just like the Fourth of July.

My dad drove an eighteen-wheeler, with short—and long-distance hauls. My parents began to incorporate taking family vacations in my freshman year of high school. I remember when my dad rented a Winnebago camper and packed us all in, and we spent two weeks on the road traveling and sightseeing different states. I never felt so alive and free. Seeing the enormous trees in Yellowstone National Park was amazing, and enjoying the beautiful sunsets in Arizona was memorable. The Grand Canyon is as majestic (just like in the pictures), and Texas (my dad's home state) and Mississippi (my mom's home state) left you feeling as if the air in those areas were from another planet, clean and fresh. While visiting relatives on their farm and witnessing how the ducks and chickens made it to the dinner table that evening was educational but was very sad, and I remember none of my younger brothers and sisters including myself were able to eat that night.

Visiting Mexico and driving across the Texas-Mexico border, my dad was able to speak Spanish with many of the locals we met along the way. Anywhere we went in Mexico, from gas stations to open markets, we experienced warm welcomes from the locals once they learned of my dad's ability to effectively communicate with them. I realized doors opened and connections were established with the ability to effectively communicate with people who are different, therefore tearing down walls of misunderstanding, breaking boundaries, and eliminating drawn lines. I traveled every summer with my family until I graduated from Jones Commercial High School; my graduation celebration included driving to Las Vegas with my mom and dad, where he allowed me to drive over one hundred miles continuously. While I drove, my dad had a conversation with me which helped me to have clarity about what I could do with my future. My dad said, "Glenda, you can go anywhere in the world you want and do anything you desire." Hearing those words had a very strong and powerful impact on me, and to this very day they inspire me when making life decisions.

This is what children (even at eighteen years old) need to hear from their parents or from anyone whom they look up to. I continued driving down the road toward Las Vegas, but I knew he was watching and making sure I didn't go over the speed limit.

CHAPTER SEVEN

The Sky Is the Limit

I thought entering Jones Commercial High School would become a special place for me. I knew of the high standards this school maintained, and it was highly visible to the business world. I was proud of the decision I had made to leave my neighborhood high school with all the loose-fitting jeans and low-cut tops that every student appeared to wear. After all, in the '70s, that was the cool way to dress. I'm not saying that the neighborhood school didn't offer anything. I'm just saying I could recognize Jones Commercial offered more for me at that time. When I spoke to some of my friends about my decision to go to Jones, their comment would almost always be "You mean that school where they wear dresses?" Or some of them didn't know of the school at all. I didn't allow their comments to discourage me, nor did I try to convince them to go, because I could see in their eyes and tone of their voices that they felt that for some reason, they were above dressing outside the current norm of the times.

Jones Commercial High School was located in the center of downtown Chicago, amid all the career opportunities, a great location for the senior students to either go to their morning jobs and then, after lunch, return to school for afternoon studies or vice versa. I had the latter schedule when I became a senior. I enjoyed that schedule and felt I gave my all to my school curriculum in the morning and had a less-controlled work environment in the afternoon.

I knew it was a special school because I witnessed my older sister graduate with a class of the most sophisticated seniors in all Chicago land. Their senior luncheon looked as if you were looking at a group of young women located in the Hamptons, with each senior wearing a hat that would remind you of being in an Easter parade. The mayor of the city of Chicago was very proud of Jones Commercial High School which dress code required that every young lady wore heels, a hat, and gloves. A dress or skirt was the only acceptable apparel, with the hemline being no higher than two inches above the knee. The last requirement was the wearing of nylon stockings every day. There was even several stocking machines located in the school to ensure if you got a run in your stockings, you could immediately replace them.

Unlike Flowers (an all-girl) High School, Jones Commercial High School (now Jones College Prep School) had approximately one hundred male students whose attire was just as "businesslike" *as the ladies*; their only acceptable attire was cardigan sweaters, if not a suit jacket or blazer. The young men could wear nothing less than suit pants or highly pressed jeans. We lived by the code of "Dress for Success," and the mayor would escort business executives and dignitaries through our model school with its modern architectural design, including six academic floors and student elevators separate from the teachers'. Having all these requirements placed on us and with the curriculum of shorthand, Dictaphone, machine transcription, and court reporting being our choice of majors, each senior class would have a 99 percent job placement average in one of the business offices downtown Chicago. I majored in machine transcription with an average typing speed of 65 wpm, and in my senior year I was placed as a clerk typist in an insurance company, located across the street from the then Sears Tower, now Willis Tower, working in the personnel department. After I graduated from Jones Commercial High School, I remained at the insurance company full-time, and I really felt blessed and special because routinely most girls who were employed went directly in the huge filing department.

On special occasions, my coworkers in personnel and I would go out for lunch together, and in the '70s, a cocktail at lunch was legal; one cocktail usually was the limit. The ladies and I would softly giggle (actually at nothing) after returning from lunch in the afternoon at our desks while we worked until the afternoon break, when it appeared the giggling urge had ceased.

After two and a half years of working as a clerk typist, I begin to speculate that if after thirty years of daily nine to five, Monday through Friday, week in and week out of working in the same setting just to receive a gold watch, possible pension, and a pat on the back, at some point, I'd begin to feel I lack job satisfaction. I felt I needed to start thinking outside the box and of a possible job or position change; after all, life was short.

CHAPTER EIGHT

Cause = Effect

While trying to assimilate in the business world, I began to tell myself to just blend in with the hustle and bustle of this beautiful city and all it seemed to offer. I slowly began to realize that I should be doing more with my life, and although I felt my past choices were good, it was only the beginning of what was to lie ahead for me. I had a close friend that had spent some time in the military; however, I had never seriously considered the military for me, nor did I really know anything about the specifics of the military. After all, my last two years of high school and work experience consisted of me being as ladylike as possible. My home life after work was spent reading and on some evenings out in the town with friends. I felt there had to be more awaiting for me in life, especially after experiencing the wide range of possibilities and freedom while away on our out-of-state family vacations.

I began to view the neighborhood, which I once considered vast, as something routine; and most of my neighbors had appeared settled in, comfortable, and even predictable.

There was one next-door neighbor I watched from a short distance who appeared to function in a very focused, independent, and "outside the box" way. He was my friend's brother, and they lived nearby on my street. I can remember him bouncing his basketball everywhere he went. If his mom sent him to the store, he would walk bouncing his basketball. He appeared average height in his earlier years, and as time went by he appeared to shoot straight up; and within several years I was looking up at him, and I stood five feet eight inches. I noticed he handled his basketball as if it were an extension of his arm, and he often played by himself for hours in his backyard and at the basketball court located in the rear of the high school across our street. I had two young male cousins approximately two years younger than my neighbor, and whenever they saw him walking with his basketball, they would yell out to him while laughing, "Can't let that basketball go," or "What's up with you and the ball?" The young man would just ignore them or give them a look of "don't bother me." One day, I was sitting on my mom's back porch and noticed the neighbor shooting hoops in his backyard. My cousins appeared in my backyard, and when they noticed the neighbor, they started heckling him; when my cousins became tired of joking on him, they turned their attention away from him, and seconds later the neighbor's basketball came hurling over the fence that separated our yards and hit one of my cousins dead center in the back of his head. I giggled, and I thought to myself, *That was an awesome thing to witness.*

I knew that the choices you make in life, provided choices are available, have a lifelong effect; and each choice you make about anything adds to your lifelong résumé. No one is perfect, and not everything you choose or place emphasis on will be correct, but whatever you do will have a direct effect on yourself and others. I feel focusing your intentions toward something better and having good intentions when making choices will make that difference in the outcome of your decision. My friend and her brother didn't have a father living in their home, but they had older brothers in the home, and it appeared to me that at an early age he had ambitions for himself and stayed focused on some goal. Today that young man has completed a professional basketball career and was able to relocate himself and his mother to a much better lifestyle and appears just as humble and focused on life as I remember him to be years ago.

I was fortunate to get one of those neighborhood summer jobs, and seizing that opportunity just as I knew that the group of kids I was working with had not been on many out-of-state trips, let alone on an aircraft; but surprisingly no one accepted our supervisor's offer, and I raised my hand to accept. I even remember after he asked again, one or two more hands were raised, but I was truly amazed at the number of refusals he got (you must first recognize an opportunity as being an option for you). I wanted to do something different, make a difference, and shoot for the stars; and since my "free airplane ride," with the president of Delta Air Lines, I found a deep admiration of aircraft and its crew members. I began to think of all the skills that it must take to master the dynamics of taking off and landing of an aircraft, and those feelings manifested only after having the opportunity to "ride free."

Those emotions I felt while working that summer later tied into my overall desire to seek a better opportunity and new career choice while employed at the insurance company.

While walking through Daley Plaza in downtown Chicago, heading toward my clerical job, I noticed a military air force recruiter, and my curiosity sent me toward his trailer to inquire about this way of life. After speaking with the recruiter and being informed by him of the opportunities in the air force and of piloting, I was already intrigued; however, he did say that entering the air force as a pilot required a four-year-college degree. He also informed me that if I chose the U.S. Army, they had a "high school to flight school" program, whereas I would have a better and faster chance at becoming pilot trained. He later guided me to an army recruiter, and that set the ball in motion. "I still had to make it to work that day." A week or so later, the army recruiter administered to me a battery of tests and informed me that my mechanical scores were very good; however, my overall score didn't qualify to enter the military as a pilot and that I can retake that overall score later while in the military doing something else. I felt that maybe this was the opportunity I needed to do something different now and yet continue to work toward the goal of becoming a pilot while becoming a part of a different group of people, servicemen and women.

So I signed up for the U.S. Army to be trained as a military policewoman with airborne qualifications, eventually after completing all the training to be stationed at Fort Bragg, North Carolina. I had met the MP qualifications: basically no previous criminal record, more so than the average enlistee, and with a height requirement of five feet six inches or taller. I had learned that the military testing system depicts what job or occupation you can be employed as. I was comfortable knowing that I could retake the test to qualify for different positions even if I changed my mind on becoming a pilot.

Joining the military was a concept that my immediate family wasn't familiar with. I was breaking new ground for the family, and I was almost certain I wanted to do this. After all I had begun a life in the city after graduating from Jones Commercial and had steady work at the insurance company. I was living on the north side of the city near the lakefront, which was exciting and versatile, and where there were great neighborhoods consisting of comfortable mixtures of different cultural people. You truly get the "moving on up" feeling with this part of town, and yet I still felt a need for change. But I felt I had to be sure, so I asked my dad an important question one evening. "Dad, do you think I should join the army?" While awaiting my dad's answer (I thought of all the documents I had already signed for entry into the service but knew I would still able to change mind), my dad replied to me just like a psychiatrist, "What do you think you should do?" I replied to him, "I think I want to join." He said nothing, and I had my answer. It took me several years to realize he was not going to tell me what I should do. It had to be my decision.

After the recruiter convincing me that signing on the dotted line would be in the best interest for me and my country and my opportunity to have a career maybe even in flying, I committed myself to three years in the military. With no former experience, no immediate family member with experience, and with no friends my age having knowledge except a close male friend who had spent less than a year in the service who commented to me, "Tell no one your secrets," I had no idea what I was really getting myself into.

I remember after leaving the military enlistee processing station (MEPS) in downtown Chicago, where I had officially started my in processing into the military by taking a physical among other things, I sat on the steps in Grant Park to reflect on everything: my job I was leaving and all my coworkers who thought I had "lost my mind" for joining the military, when this young lady sat down fairly close to me, and we began talking. It was a nice summer day, and everything was so green; the grass and trees smelled so good, and I told her, "I just joined the army," and the girl replied to me, "You poor thing." I said to her quietly, "I think I will be all right."

CHAPTER NINE

Entering the Military

It was official; I was in the army now. I entered the military in 1978, and I was to report to Fort McClellan, Alabama, located just outside Anniston, Alabama. The first thing for every new soldier (yes, that was awkward to hear as my new title) was to negotiate initial basic training, and for my contract with the military service, military police school would immediately follow basic training at the same location, and my initial entry training would culminate at Fort Benning, Georgia, for airborne training (jump school). Leaving Chicago via aircraft followed by a bus ride through what appeared to be a rural area of Alabama, I became aware there were other new enlistees besides myself on the bus, so I didn't feel so alone on the trip to my new temporary home.

Once we reached our destination and the bus stopped on base, the bus door opened, and there stood a sergeant in uniform, with a wide-brimmed brownish-green military hat on his head (later I learned that color, very common in the army, to be OD green), and his first words to us were "Come on off the bus, and get in line." He didn't appear too frightening as long as you follow every order he gave you to the letter.

After they made sure we were who we were supposed to be, our next stop was to get in processed and get our "new wardrobe". I really couldn't believe we had to wear those pants and boots every day, but after several days there, I realized that was the only outfit everyone wore all the time, and I began to notice the more tailored and impressive ones from others. Our housing was a dormlike dwelling, a fairly new facility and air-conditioned. It was probably our housing building that was the sole thing that taught most of us how to become team players because we did not have maids; we had to keep our own billets well maintained. The areas of our responsibility included buffing the floors and cleaning the bathroom which had about ten toilets; requiring everyone to pitch in to keep them clean, or we would all get some kind of demerit and lose privileges of having a candy bar or some kind of recognition. After four weeks of no sodas and junk food, only healthy eating, you would do anything for a candy bar.

Fort McClellan was quite different from city life, but anyone who has travelled anywhere outside the city limits of Chicago would know that we have a lot of farmland nearby also, but Alabama felt different; and thinking back, it was probably the dialect that most Alabamians have that made me seem farther away from home than I really was. I realized after being stationed at Fort McClellan for several days that the dialect emphasizes all the vowels which are strong in words, such as "like" and "good." The locals pronounce those words similar to how these words look: "gooood" or "liiiiike," and the same with the *E* and *I*. So I realized *A, E, I, O, U,* and sometimes *Y* will always be emphasized when they spoke. You get used to it after a while, but it still felt like *Green Acres* sometimes.

I remember one day while we were freezing in our very air-conditioned dorm, I decided to open the main door to the outside to let some warm air in. The girls seemed very appreciative to me for doing that, and it actually started to feel nice inside. One of our drill sergeants (every company of soldiers had two or three to train you from day 1 until graduation) came walking through the door, and he shouted, "Who is trying to cool off lower Alabama?" (Just upon him entering our dorm put us at the position of attention and positioned at the foot of our beds). I replied, "I did, Drill Sergeant." He walked over to me and stood only inches from my face and said, "Why"? I told him why and he then said these words to me that has helped me throughout my life. He said, "You had good initiative but bad judgment. Keep the door shut!" My first thought was he didn't have to yell, and then I thought I didn't display "common sense." Suddenly, I felt something I hadn't felt in a long time, and that was the feeling I got when I knew my mother was analyzing and teaching me how to think on my feet. I actually appreciated his candor, but I couldn't figure out what all the yelling was about.

Basic training was interesting because they taught us how to walk all over again. I thought I knew my left foot from my right, but walking in unison and turning in the same manner is actually difficult.

Basic training seemed to last forever, but it was only eight weeks of training, which consisted of map reading, weapons training, and first aid. You probably ask yourself, "Why first aid?" It was so we can help keep each another alive if wounded until help arrive. So in essence, we received medical training. Weapons training was intense, and we became familiar with several pieces of equipment along with cleaning them. I believe the hand grenade was very interesting and is a very dangerous device. In my opinion, these military weapons have no place on the city streets, and somehow people are walking around with these weapons and obviously in their minds it's okay. These weapons need to be handled under strict supervision, and I wonder about the Humvee also. I still don't understand why anyone would need that kind of vehicle in the city. That's like having a Corvette in an Amish community.

I was aware of the height requirement for becoming an MP, and I knew that would be no problem for me because I was over five feet eight inches and the tallest girl in my immediate family. I do believe I received my height from my grandmother on my mother's side, as she stood quite tall and of status and, as I remember now, was quite loved and respected by many. My main concern in becoming an MP was more serious than how tall I was; it was the weapons issue, and before entering the military, I had confided in my sister, "I don't want to have to kill anyone." So you may ask, "Why join the army?" I knew I was taking a chance in joining the military and anything was possible, but life is about choices and also the courage to take chances (with good judgment). And after, my sister simply said to me, "You won't," and I never did, in my entire military career.

Grandmother

Overall basic training was very interesting and good training to sustain a new soldier until they reach their permanent unit to begin more intense training.

My military job specialty, military policewoman (MP) was at the same location, same dorm, and essentially the same girls I basic trained with, except for two female marines we had moved into our dorms for MP training because the marines didn't have the provisions to accommodate women for that particular career field. I was totally impressed with their demeanor and their uniforms; even their hats were starched and crisp. We thought we had learned a few things, until they arrived, but we all worked well together.

The MP training lasted approximately eight weeks, which included intense training with hand-to-hand combat, more weapons training, and shoot, no shoot mock-ups. We were slowly gaining more freedom on base and received occasional passes to go into town; it was as if they didn't trust us to know how to behave, and I can understand that because many soldiers were just eighteen years old.

We maintained the same two drill sergeants throughout basic and MP school training, and upon our completion of both courses, we had the greatest admiration for both of them because we were totally unaware of anything upon arriving there; and in the time span of sixteen weeks, we were just beginning to transform into something special for our future units.

CHAPTER TEN

Jump School

Leaving Fort McClellan was inviting, and at the same time, I knew I had my hands full with what was yet to come. I had learned from many of the drill sergeants in basic training that airborne school was nothing to take lightly. I had wanted to return home to Chicago to visit my family that I had not seen for over sixteen weeks. It seemed I had become a different person, and I felt a need to reconnect with them; and conversing with many of the other soldiers in my company, I found that they all felt the same way, but the drill sergeants warned me in particular against it. One drill sergeant spoke candidly with me and said, "Don't go home now that you have been trained and you're ready for more rigorous training, because you will need everything you've got to complete that course." He said that if I go home now and go back to drinking sodas and possibly alcohol and not getting enough rest, I will not complete U.S. Army Airborne training, and I would literally have to be retrained as hard as basic training before tackling the airborne course.

I had no doubt in believing this sergeant. I sensed he wanted me to have the best advantage in taking on this next challenge. After learning the history of the military and the purpose of the army and its commitment to excellence with any mission or task that it undertakes, whether as a group or as an individual, we as individual soldiers were all linked together; we were a team, and each one of us is a part of something bigger than ourselves. I was really beginning to feel the esprit de corps.

So I took his advice and went straight from Alabama to the Airborne Training Center in Fort Benning, Georgia, even though I really wanted to go home.

To add to my worry about not seeing my family before taking on this new challenge, which was just days away from me beginning, I began to focus on the obvious different levels of danger airborne training would encompass than the two previous schools I had just graduated from. When I told my mom that I would be soon jumping from an aircraft, my mom simply asked, "From how high, Glenda?" I learned to really appreciate her statement because I really needed her support even though I know she was worried about me attending the school.

Arriving at Fort Benning, Georgia, which was located just outside Columbus, Georgia, I realized that all of these southern states have the freshest-smelling air, and you can appreciate the thought of hanging freshly washed laundry outside to dry in this air. After getting settled in my two-man room (moving on up in military life), I found out that my class would start in approximately one week, so I was in what they called zero week of a three-week course.

Always physical training

I was in a class of over 250 men and only twenty-one women, enlisted personnel and officers combined. Our class had an overwhelming number of officers because, I later learned, that the military looks favorably to soldiers (officers and enlisted) with this airborne qualifier. It was encouraged for officers to try to complete this course because it also became a tool for the Department of the Army to use for decision making in who to promote and not because of the intense training, courage, and motivation it takes to complete it. Most soldiers quickly decline any opportunity to attend this particular training.

Our training began in the early mornings, well before sunrise, and I remember standing with my helmet on, my head hidden as an individual in rows of other candidates like myself, probably wondering what the heck was I was doing there. As I waited for the ground week black hat instructors (that's what they were called because they wore black caps) to complete the roll call by calling each soldier's number, I would occasionally allow myself to lose my focus on the current situation (only after my number, W9—the *W* was a phonetic identifier used for the women attending the course—was called) and take a minute to enjoy the view of the dark morning sky with the stars still present from the night prior and a few seconds more to listen for the sounds of birds nearby, which would surely be annoyed by all the commotion that we were creating that early in the morning. I used to think we were up before the birds arose.

Every day, we had the same routine for ground week, beginning with roll call, followed by physical training, which included a pretty fast-paced run in combat boots and in formation. Formation running was introduced to me in basic training; that is just how the military does it, uniform and organized, instead of looking like a cluster of people making different moves and eventually becoming a mob running in the streets. This fashion of running also allowed the instructors to know if a soldier was not keeping pace because in order to fall back, you had to fall out, or else you would create a massive chain reaction of an unorganized appearance and create a gap for everyone running behind you and the elements of the formation directly in front of you. For us women, the pace was always too fast; however, if the entire group was slowed just for the benefit of having a suitable women's pace, it always hindered the males' stride and was not within the established time limit of the run. Many of the men would complain of shin splints if the pace dropped below a particular speed, so it always felt as if we ran like Kentucky horses—fast.

We knew from the beginning of this course that not every airborne candidate would complete this course, and for us women, the runs were our major contributor to this. Not only did we have the challenge of keeping up with the pace of the run, but we also sung as we ran. The songs we sang at that time in the military were called "Jody Calls." One person, either an instructor or if a candidate felt confident enough to lead the group in song, would run alongside of the formation, calling out lyrics; and the group would mimic the call. The Jody Call will make you laugh and think while running. That alone was exhausting, but I later learned that if I paced myself and used the song as a method of controlling my breathing, most of the run was mind over matter, provided that you were physically fit. That is when I soon realized that the drill sergeant who warned me not to go home had his reasons. As we ran, we sang, "C-130 rolling down the strip, airborne soldier going to take a little trip, stand up, hook up, shuffle to the door, jump right out, and count to four." This song was one of many that we would sing on these runs, obviously to keep up morale and stride; also, the running help to build our endurance and leg strength, which was an important element in making a safe foot landing with a parachute.

The black hats were very professional at all times, as in keeping with the standards of the U.S. Army, and we always address them in a professional manner even when we were not in the training mode; but at any time, if they felt you had fallen too far back in the run, from 50 to 100 ft. from the main formation element, they would declare that you have finished your run, and you would be considered a "dropout" of that particular run; and you were only allowed two in the entire three-week course.

The physical training portion of the day was just ending as the sun was rising, and then it was time for personal hygiene, followed by breakfast, and by 10:00 a.m., we were ready for the real training, thus the term "we do more before 10:00 a.m. than most people do all day." Most airborne classes always included several riggers whose military occupation was reconfiguring parachutes and packing them into the chute holders, and this included our reserve pack that we wore on the front of our body during jumps. The reserve is only utilized if in the unlikely event that our main parachute does not open; you rip off the side of its carrier and begin to toss your chute out in the correct manner as to not get tangled into it and become a human torpedo heading toward ground. For riggers, jump school was a mandatory to attend and pass because they also had to jump with the parachutes they packed.

Ground week also consisted of learning the different types of parachutes, history of the airborne soldier, and their campaigns and the "mock door" practice of overcoming the fear of jumping out of an aircraft without actually seeing something underneath you to catch you as you fall; it was mental. That proved to be a factor in successfully making a safe aircraft door departure and also led to many soldiers being eliminated due to unsafe behavior. This term "unsafe behavior" was used throughout the course to eliminate individuals who were just not assimilating to the overall course and would be deemed unsafe for themselves or others to continue.

Teaching us how to land on the ground with the parachute was a hard task to complete for many of the candidates because if the landing, called the parachute landing fall (PLF), was not correct, there was a high probability of you either breaking or spraining a leg, if not both. By the end of ground week, we had lost slightly less than one-third of the entire class due to many of the candidates receiving unsatisfactory PLFs.

During ground week alone, we lost over half of the twenty-one female candidates, mainly because of the physical training run.

CHAPTER ELEVEN

Tower Week

Entering tower week was a welcomed change, and I began to feel as if we were getting closer to the goal of jumping; we had learned about all the aircraft we could engage with, and I felt I couldn't have been in better shape.

The towers we would be training on stood approximately 250 ft. tall with four arms at the top, where parachutes were attached, and at the signal one at a time, the parachute would detach, and you would float to the surface. Upon reaching the ground, you perform your PLF and recover the parachute. This part of training was the closest to actually knowing what it felt and what it looked like up in the air and the dynamics of floating in the air. I was starting to become excited over the idea of parachuting, and it no longer seemed far-fetched but more like a sporting event to me. I knew I had to stay focused, because I had learned of all the things that could go wrong on a jump, but the odds of something happening was rare, so I knew I had to continue on with what I had started with the course; after all, I was close to being the sole woman left in my class. We had only two women left by mid-tower week because the physical training runs were continuing to take a toll on our group of female candidates; they were literally falling out of runs left and right. I was thankful that prior to me physically entering the service, I began running in my neighborhood with a girlfriend to condition myself for basic training, and I realized that my overall preparation and not going home were paying off.

By the end of tower week, the runs were very intense. I wasn't so sure anymore if I would make the end of the week without falling out also because I had started getting shin splints. And I knew that the guys had picked up the pace because there were only two females left in the class, and they were starting to gain momentum. Their strides were long and fast, coupled with the boots; that really made it tough for me to keep up, and then the other female fell back. I yelled to her to come up to where I was, but she couldn't. I knew she had given out, and when the black hat began to run back toward her to make sure she was okay (and then she began to walk), I knew it was over for her. I was officially the last female left in my class, and then something happened; one of the black hats began to run by my side, and I will never forget his words of encouragement to me. The black hat yelled to me, "Don't fall out, Whiskey. You're the last one left. Don't stop now." And I knew that these instructors were very partial to all the soldiers and that he knew I wanted this with all my might, and he broke silence to give me that little push to make it. And with that, I picked up my head and increased my speed to fall in just to the rear of the last soldier running.

CHAPTER TWELVE

Jump Week

Entering jump week seemed like a dream. I had little time to reflect too long on the fact that I was the only female left in my class. Jump week had specific requirements that had to be met to be considered graduation ready and airborne qualified: there had to be five jumps made, and two of the jumps had to be combat ready, and that meant full combat gear. Also, two of the five jumps were to be made in the nighttime. I had begun to have some anxiety over the entire actual jumping process, but I was going with the flow and was, at that point, determined to finish this course. I also knew that if I didn't complete the course, I would have broken my initial contract with the army to become an airborne MP; thus the military, in all fairness, could ship me anywhere they pleased and for the needs of the army. I knew this meant I could have been shipped overseas—Korea, Germany, and possibly Timbuktu; so I knew I had to finish this.

Jump Committee

Our first jump was going to be on a C-130 military air force aircraft. The C-130 aircraft is one of the oldest aircraft in the air force fleet—very durable and was used for cargo and troop transportation. The instructors for jump week were called jumpmasters; these soldiers had a long history of airborne training and had to have over fifty jumps to even think about becoming a jumpmaster. Once we boarded the aircraft and were seated, the jumpmaster began to let us know that he was the only one giving orders on his aircraft, and we were to follow each order to the T. I wasn't afraid on this jump; it was the ones to follow. Once we were in the air, the jumpmaster informed us, "No one is going to land with this aircraft," and when the green light came on, I knew it was where the "rubber would meet the road." This jump should be a good one because we were jumping out without full gear, and we called that a Hollywood jump (meaning it could get no better than this). The jumpmaster had given us all the commands to safely exit the aircraft. "Outboard personnel, stand up," followed by all the formal commands to safely get us to that green-lit doorframe. Once we were standing in the aircraft and the parachutes were hooked up to the steel cable support line on board and the green light came on, indicating we were over the drop zone, everything began to happen quickly. There was the first jumper that was ordered to "stand in the door," and with that command, that jumper would turn toward the open door and place his hands on the doorframe for support and await the jumpmaster's command to say "go." With that command, the jumper at the door would exit the aircraft, and the rest of the jumpers would literally rush to the door and had very little time to think before we were out of that door.

Exiting the aircraft to the time of ground impact lasted no more than ten minutes. Once I hit that door, it felt as if I was being sucked out of it, and I immediately went into the body positions I had been taught. I began my count to ensure that I monitored the time of exit until the time my parachute opened. Once my parachute opened, I relaxed and tried to enjoy the ride down from approximately 2,000 to 1,500 ft. Everything went as safe as expected; now on to jump 2, which was scheduled for that afternoon.

Preparing for the second jump, I realized a difference in the guys' behavior. They appeared more apprehensive, as I knew I was feeling that way also. The aircraft was quiet. That first jump was an eye-opener, and I knew everyone sensed the real danger in the entire process, so all the eagerness was replaced with a little fear. While in the aircraft and flying toward the drop zone, the jumpmaster did something none of us expected; he yelled, "Whiskey 9," and with his command, I turned my attention toward him and answered, "Yes, Jumpmaster?" And he replied, "Unhook and come up here." Everyone turned and looked at me, and after I had made my way to where he was standing, which was by the door, he said, "Stand in the door". I looked at him and said, "What did I do?" He didn't change his expression or the command, and I slowly turned and looked out at the open sky and looked back at him, and he repeated the command to me. I remember slowly and mechanically turning toward the door and placing my hands on the door as we had been taught in ground week. I knew what he was doing; he was going to show those guys that if this girl can go, their ego would not let me show them up by him having to remind any of them that the aircraft was flying home solo. When the light above the door turned green, he yelled at me to go, and I just looked at him, and I knew from the look on his face he was not going to negotiate with me on this. He repeated the command, and I saw myself turning, and I closed my eyes and jumped. Once outside of the aircraft, I opened my eyes; and as I saw that magnificent huge aircraft looming past me, I closed my eyes again until I felt the tug of my parachute. As I floated toward the ground, I looked around and saw several of the guys nearby, and we spoke to one another to ensure we maintained distance and made sure we were okay. Then came the landing.

After that incident on the aircraft, I knew I was officially part of the team; I felt that the guys had a different respect for me, even though if I had my choice in the matter, I would have turned around in that aircraft and gone back to my original seat regardless of what he was saying. I really didn't want to hear it, but it paid off to take that chance and leap of faith.

On our third jump, we had another female join us to complete her last jump; she had to stand down for some medical reason during her class, and they allowed her to finish her last jump with our class. I figured they knew she was a good candidate and had made it that far; why not let her finish? I welcomed another female; maybe she would get to stand in the door.

Our night jump was as intense as it sounds; we really couldn't see a thing, and you could barely make out the treetops in the dark as you're descending into them; some of the guys became tangled into them, but somehow I did well with that jump also. It wasn't until my last jump that I hit the ground hard and ended my course with a slight limp. I remember with every jump, I prayed hard to safely complete each jump, and I was so thankful to God that he allowed me to complete that course in the fashion that I did and without real harm.

We graduated on the DZ (drop zone), and with a press of our silver wings on our chest, we received what many airborne soldiers know as blood wings. The formal part of the ceremony placed us in the bleachers because we celebrated outside, and we were all dusty, all 175 of us; then something else amazed me. As they began to announce the honor student, in which every military class gives honor to a student that exceeded the standards and rose above everyone else, I sat and listened as everyone else because I was starting to limp and was just very happy to be down and safe and have officially completed the course. What happened next amazed me; when the announcer paused before saying the name of the candidate, half the class turned and looked over to me where I sat; and as he called the young male soldier's name, I felt I had already received my accolades from at least half of my class. *Airborne*!

CHAPTER THIRTEEN

Fort Bragg, North Carolina

Upon completing jump school, I stayed at Fort Benning for one additional week to allow my sprain to heal. The black hats appeared to be very happy with me and with my accomplishment of first completing the course, and second, some of the black instructors made it clear to me that they were proud to see one of their own complete the course. The administration director informed me that I could stay the week, rest up, and I can walk tall to my next duty station. That time, without any scheduled activities, allowed me to get plenty of relaxation and healing time that I needed for my sprained ankle. I took long cleansing and thought-provoking walks through nearby woods and took plenty of photos of the beautiful scenery on that base.

I learned by the end of the week that I would be leaving Fort Benning, Georgia, and heading inbound to my permanent duty station, Fort Bragg, North Carolina, (Home of the airborne), located just outside of Fayetteville, North Carolina. I had orders to be stationed at the 118th MP Company (airborne), and I recently learned while watching the movie *Green Zone*, the 118th MP Company was briefly shown in the picture.

This company had a prestigious history and just as most of only the airborne units located on Fort Bragg; the unit wore berets (our unit color was maroon, and Special Forces' was black) instead of the typical army cap that nonjump-status soldiers donned. Approximately 75 percent of the soldiers stationed at Fort Bragg were airborne qualified. I was not aware of anything about this unit until I actually arrived there.

Upon arriving at my new unit, I was greeted by company officials and personnel; and because this unit hadn't recently experienced having women assigned to their unit, they didn't have living provisions for me at their company area. I was going to live in the much larger female barracks of the 503rd MP Battalion, which was located just down the same street that the 118th MP Company was located. I was actually breaking new ground at this particular company, as I was truly the first black female (airborne) MP soldier assigned to this unit. This lack of preparation and accommodation for women at this company and many others with combat emphasis was directly correlated to the fact that the army had just recently within the year disbanded the separate and distinct Women's Army Corps (WACs). The WACs was an all female organization separate of the army, thus allowing women to serve their country if they chose to; and with the WACs' recent integration into the Department of the Army, most all-men units were still trying to adapt to accommodating newly assigned women.

Being stationed at the 118th MP Company, the guys in the unit went out of their way to help me assimilate with all the requirements of the unit; and when it was time for my first jump with the company, it was called my cherry jump. The company had a tradition for their new paratroopers to wear a helmet painted all white with red cherries on it.

The guys were proud of me, and I was proud of my unit. The unit captain and first sergeant were very distinguished black men and had lots of military experience.

All-Female Parachute Jump, Fort Bragg, 1980, compliments of the *Fayetteville Observer*

Women hail anniversary

by Larry White

The sun began its steady descent into the horizon behind them. While the setting sun represented the end of another work day for some, it signaled the beginning of another night of duty for these soldiers.

Several parts of intentive ears listened as the platoon sergeant gave them their final instructions. One particular pair of ears belonged to a soldier unique to this 118th Military Police Company (Airborne). Those ears belonged to Private First Class Glenda Dugar, the lone woman 118th MP to participate in joint training exercise Solid Shield 79.

"Challenge everyone and handle yourselves in a professional manner. Stay on your toes," the platoon sergeant ordered.

In a sense different from what the platoon sergeant meant, a challenge has always attracted Dugar. A challenge lured Dugar, from her Chicago home to the U.S. Army almost a year ago. She later graduated from airborne training and was assigned to the 118th MP Co.

The 118th MP Co. has an active role in Solid Shield 79 and Dugar is one of several U.S. Army female soldiers to perform vital missions to the overall success of the maneuvers.

Women in the Army received official recognition on May 14, 1942, and later became the Women's Army Corp (WAC). Although the WAC is now defunct, it provided the impetus for the woman to have an even greater opportunity to perform jobs for years reserved for the man.

From cooks, to drivers, to draftsmen, to clerks, to military police persons, the woman is active in the Army.

Dugar, the military police person whose position was spawned from the WAC, downplays her involvement in the unit. "We're somewhat of a unique unit," she said. "We're all just friends. We like working together -- regardless of sex."

Many of the male members of Dugar's unit say her being a woman has presented no adverse problems. "She does her job and so far we've had no complaints," one sergeant said. A lieutenant added, "It's probably more of a problem for her because she's a woman and many of the guys refuse to recognize that she succeeded in finishing jump school. It diminishes their macho image."

None of those opinions phase Dugar, whose only problem while participating in Solid Shield may be establishing billeting separate from her male co-workers.

"You're only as good as you want to be," Dugar declared. "I just want to be happy. I'm happy now. I have other goals but I'm happy."

When Dugar arrived to the 118th Mp. Co. in October she did not think she would be the only female in the unit. She was. Until recently that distinction remained. Now, another female has joined the ranks.

On being in a field environment, Dugar has experienced no apparent difficulties. "We go if the general goes," she said when asked how often she is deployed to a field location.

During Solid Shield 79, Dugar's unit provides internal and Mobile Strategic Command Post (MOBSTRAC) security and VIP escort, along with several other responsibilities.

When she dones her gear she becomes "one of the guys."

As the sun seeks cover, Dugar is deployed on patrol, a 12 - hour stint that taxes the mind and body. The rigors of the assignments don't bother her because it's "the thought of doing something challenging."

There's Something

For Everyone

in

The Paraglide

Courtesy of the *Paraglide*

Our post-physical training run days where the entire post ran was very organized; even our military police dogs ran in formation with us. It was actually something to see, and for at least four miles of running (a much slower pace than jump school)—with unit formation after unit in line, in unison with guidon bearers holding their unit designation flag leading their formation along with their unit commander—it was exhilarating.

There was a section of the base called COSCOM where mainly nonairborne soldiers worked and lived and who performed administrative functions. We had a name for nonairborne soldiers, which was the word "legs"—which meant basically the soldiers' legs never left the ground.

My unit and I jumped often, more than I had desired because my desire to pursue flying had not changed, and I figured I had to wait for the right time to do that. My career field job of military police was just like any other eight-hour shift, sometimes twelve hours, depending on what base mission was in progress. Fort Bragg was a post with certain units, always ready to deploy at any time, anywhere, around the world, because of the Special Forces, Green Berets, and the Eighty-second Airborne units being stationed there. It's a post that maintains a high state of readiness, a highly trained combat post. I knew that I needed to wait a while to try to change my career field for piloting.

The 118th MPs would occasionally receive out-of-country and state missions, but normally not as a complete unit. One of our main important missions was to guard and protect the post in general; however, sometimes select soldiers were tasked to certain away jobs.

It was not long before the unit received another airborne female MP soldier, and I welcomed her. We became close friends as expected because there weren't many of our kind on post. Soon thereafter, we had a female supply clerk and cook, who were also airborne qualified, enter our unit.

The guys in my unit loved playing pranks on new paratroopers, and while I was still the only female in the unit, I wasn't excluded from this pleasure of theirs. One day not too long after I had arrived at 118th MP Company, myself and another newly arrived soldier was told in a very serious manner to go to the provost marshal office (PMO, commander of the MP station) to retrieve the keys to the drop zone. Upon letting his secretary know that we were there to see the colonel for the key pickup, we were allowed back to his office. We both stood in front of his desk and at parade rest (hands folded behind our backs and feet spread slightly apart), we got the colonel's attention, and he looked up from his work, and we said almost simultaneously, "Sir, we are here to pick up the keys to the drop zone." The colonel's eyebrows went up, and he yelled, "Get out of here." Almost instantly, we heard giggles from the outside of his office door, and then we realized we had been pranked. There are no keys to an open sandy field.

While stationed in the 118th MP Company and working side by side of some of the finest military policemen and (women), I was being trained constantly by my partner that had many years of MP experience. One evening while on duty, my partner, an older sergeant, drove me to the base housing section and pointed out to me a boarded-up house quarter of the physician who had lived there and had a case pending for murdering his family; he claimed a group of hippies had broken into his home while he was not there and murdered his wife and kids. This story was later made into a film and shown on television.

The seriousness of being a paratrooper was profound, and that was made clear to all after a captain's parachute did not open, and he did what we paratroopers call a cigarette roll all the way down, only to bounce off the ground several times; it was very sobering to hear of his fate. It was later found out that his parachute cord had been cut, and this is another reason why riggers must also jump with parachutes that they pack.

In contemplating what might have been the captain's final moments, I knew that his reaction time was short; from the moment he realized his chute was not going to open (with a delay of a chute opening over ten seconds for aircraft and longer for helicopters), he probably panicked. We learned that he did not attempt to open his reserve parachute located on his front abdomen area and was more than likely in a state of shock all the way down until impact.

While sitting at his memorial service and staring at his helmet and boots placed on the stage symbolic to his person, it was very sobering, and I was beginning to realize I was going to need a change in lifestyle.

I wasn't ready to give up my jumping career just yet, but I was seriously considering it. I found myself eager to participate in the military's first "all-female" parachute jump with a female airborne general leading us. That was exciting and groundbreaking, and we all landed safely and enjoyed the day together.

At Fort Bragg, North Carolina, the sun setting over the horizon at the end of the day was a beautiful thing to witness, and sometimes my friends and I would go for walks just to catch a glimpse of this beautiful event. Our fellow MP soldiers on duty driving around would stop by and chat with us, and if we had the opportunity to temporary acquire (steal) their jeep or vehicle just to have them chase us, we would, giggling all the way for a short block, maybe two. We played our pranks too.

The 503rd MP Battalion had over five hundred military policemen and women assigned to it, but they were nonairborne (legs) soldiers. The mission of the 503rd MPs was impressive also, and the battalion consisted of three individual companies, all of which had different missions; and those units frequently traveled out of state and country on real world missions and many times in support of the president of the United States. I soon began to realize how much travel and training the battalion was giving its soldiers mainly because I still resided there since my arrival to the post, and many of the conversations I had with the 503rd MP girls explained in much detail the jobs and commitments they were experiencing. I soon began to think that the "legs had more fun," and maybe it was time for that change. So after serving my unit 118th MP on several missions, field problems, and duty patrol, I decided to put my wings to rest—but not the identifier, which was now an official part of my uniform—and join the 503rd MP Battalion (Leg Land).

I knew that I had made a good decision because the first mission I accompanied the 503rd Battalion on after I left the 118th MPs was in support of our then president of the U.S. at his inauguration as crowd control and support of the local police in Washington DC. Other missions I experienced with the 503rd included crowd control at West Point, New York, for the cadets' graduation with the U.S. president as guest speaker. As I watched him speak from the grassy area I was situated on, I remember thinking how I could have never been closer to this man under any other circumstance. One challenging mission that most of the battalion was detailed for was the in processing of Castro-ousted citizens who were being held in camps located in Fort Indiantown Gap, Pennsylvania, which was depicted in the movie *Scarface*.

Overall, my new unit involved a variety of traveling missions, and I was able to travel home as time permitted and my leave allowed. I knew I had made the correct choice.

CHAPTER FOURTEEN

Everyone Makes Mistakes

I eventually retook the military FAST test for the purpose of completing my packet for submission for pilot training and scored well enough this time on the examination to pursue just about any occupational course the military offers. My focus was to get my flight packet submitted to the Department of the Army for review as soon as possible. I had more than a good chance of being selected by the review board to be awarded the school because my record was flawless, actually exceptional for a woman. One day while in the 503rd MP Battalion area, I made a costly mistake and took a sergeant's order to report to the motor pool (military vehicles and equipment holding area) lightly. He was my sergeant and also casual friend—nothing more—and I thought I had a little more time to react to his order. That decision I made to report later than he expected proved to be very costly to me. He reported my late arrival to the commander. Some things are unbeatable, and I was reprimanded for that behavior. That report was also included in my military records, as most information good or bad is, and the results of that action adversely affected my packet for request for pilot training. I realized my dream of becoming a pilot was not an immediate option anymore. The board stated that I could reapply at a later date.

I was afforded the opportunity to change career fields (except for pilot—that was a special request process) if I decided to reenlist (three years had already passed).

The current U.S. president had warned the civilian striking air traffic controllers (ATC) to return to work, or they would be fired. The civilian air traffic controllers refused, and the president of the U.S. relieved them of their jobs. So that was my choice, with a cash bonus for reenlistment for military ATC. Many military ATCs replaced the fired civilian controllers, and of course the field opened up with a huge need, and that's where I fit in. My test score had already qualified me for the school, so I reported to Fort Rucker, Alabama, for training. Many state troopers were also looking for MPs departing the service and would come to the battalion looking for new recruits, but I knew I had enough of crime fighting.

I know many people ask the question, "Why reenlist?" Wasn't three years enough? Haven't you had enough of those boots? What are you thinking? I even thought it over, and I came to realize that the military lifestyle was becoming a part of me. I actually enjoyed the thrill of it and also being a part of the military's mission and our strong connection and ties with the president of the U.S., who was ultimately in charge. I knew this was a special organization with special people willing to make any sacrifice for the mission at a moment's notice, and I was having fun.

I remember one evening after the girls and I had finished eating a large pizza, we took the box and decided to give "Iron Mike" a specific job title. Iron Mike was located at the post entrance in the middle of the highway. He stood over 30 ft. tall, with one arm leaning on his knee and an M16 in his other shoulder. He stood guarding the post entrance and represented every soldier. The pizza was good, and so with a full belly, we low crawled to Iron Mike to avoid detection of our fellow MPs that was on duty heading to and from post and managed to strap the huge box that we had turned into an armband with the words "MP" written on his arm that was propped up on his knee. We heard at roll the next morning that the colonel had said, "Get that off of him." We thought he looked good.

CHAPTER FIFTEEN

Plenty Romance, Little Love

I remember my mom once telling me, "Glenda, no two people love each other the same." I have come to realize that if you decide to choose to fall in love with a person, try to choose one who loves you more than you love them; this way, they will at least meet you halfway.

My son was born at Fort Bragg military hospital, and his birth changed everything in my life. I love being a mother, and I knew he was my legacy. I remained in the service of the military; it was my choice, even with a family.

My reenlistment for ATC school sent me to Fort Rucker, Alabama, located outside of Daleville, Alabama. And I had an exciting feeling of knowing that I was becoming more affiliated with aircraft, and after completion of ATC school, I would be officially part of one of the army's newest branches, known as army aviation. This post trained pilots, air traffic controllers, and flight operations specialists, among other specialties. I met many friends while training there, and upon graduation of this course, I knew I would be heading overseas to South Korea, the "Land of the Calm."

After arriving in South Korea, I realized just how amazing their culture was—almost a culture shock, but in a good way. There was a lot to adapt to and have respect for: the people, food, and lots of fun. My ATC duties were exciting there, and the heliport was located in the nearby town outside of the post, so I rode my bicycle to and from post to get to work every day. On days when the weather was nice, I walked and enjoyed the sights of the village. My post was located many miles from the 38th parallel, but the nearby town and post had a curfew of 11:00 p.m. to not be on the streets, and that was for everyone's safety.

While in Korea, I visited the demilitarized zone (DMZ) 38th parallel. I visited it as a tourist, but we had to be in uniform. The tour provided us with detailed information of the history of previous incidents, with pictures; it was apparent that there is danger at that location and beyond. The negotiation table that is utilized at that location rests on the center dividing line between the North and South Korean borders, and when deliberating, neither party should cross the table. This manner of communication between both sides still exists today.

The U.S. President created a "drug free" military, and that included no more beers at lunch and happy hours. That behavior was becoming frowned upon. Testing for drugs became routine in the military, and there was only one time to make that mistake of coming up positive on a test; that would ultimately lead to a soldier's out processing of the military. So I can truly say I knew that military personnel were "drug free," and if not, they were eventually caught and processed out of the military.

DMZ conference table

City of Uijongbu, Korea

La Guardia Heliport Tower

I had an opportunity to fly a helicopter in Korea (no landing nor taking off); a pilot friend allowed me to experience the thrill of the joystick and reporting over the microphone on one of the checkpoints the pilots used to give us controllers the location of their whereabouts. That was fun, especially when the controller on duty recognized my voice.

I had dorm friends, many of which I saw at my next duty station upon my departure from Korea.

CHAPTER SIXTEEN

Fort Campbell, Kentucky

"Home of the Screaming Eagles." I was stationed here with a company of men and women air traffic controllers after returning from Korea. Fort Campbell, Kentucky, specialized in air assault training and certification, which involved repelling out and down Black Hawk helicopters or other aircraft hovering over you. You can imagine the rotor wash and noise; however, staying calm was essential to conducting these operations.

Kentucky is another beautiful state. We spent many hours outdoors either working or cleaning equipment. Taking in the fresh air while training was always rewarding, and thinking about it, sometimes just working outdoors on a nice summer day was nice. Our portable towers that we used for field duty and its supporting machinery took lots of maintenance. But we had a day set aside just for that: motor pool day.

We received an alert for Afghanistan during the same time as a Black Hawk was downed in Somalia. (now a movie). I remember some of the soldiers who had much combat experience voicing to me how they will try to take their own weapons and knives to Afghanistan if they were deployed, other than what our unit provided. I could only picture the confusion that it would cause and the danger it could place on other soldiers, not to mention the soldiers attempting to utilize their own weapons.

I realized my military career was building, and it was no longer just a job—it had become a career. I kept a small card in my wallet that read, "I am God, and I am with thee." I would always refer to this card just to keep those words in my heart and keep my spirit high because all these career adventures were still very dangerous.

CHAPTER SEVENTEEN

Military Overseas Living

I was finally deployed to Europe. I thought that was the last place (besides Korea) I wanted to be. It turned out to be just the opposite. Being stationed in Europe, just outside of Nuremberg, Germany, was unbelievable. The food, history, and architecture of the city were remarkable. The Europeans have a great way of combining the old structure and building new, but they both work together and continue to give you the old-world charm about the place.

I had never seen original castles before (other than Disneyland's), and the knowledge of the age of these dwellings makes you realize just how old of a European country Germany is. The currency at that time was the deutsche mark (now part of the euro), and that was two marks to one dollar and meant lots of good spending for traveling U.S. personnel. The time has since changed with the value of our currency, and it is almost a total reverse.

Europe meant lots of concerts and traveling to nearby France and East and West Berlin. East Berlin had the panda bear before we had even seen a live one in the U.S. We entered through the famous Checkpoint Charlie military police checkpoint; that was the only entryway into West Berlin and it existed for many years prior the recently torn-down wall which divided the two sides.

Checkpoint Charlie gate entrance into West Berlin

Panda bear at Berlin Zoo

City building of Berlin

My military mission in Germany was air traffic control (I almost forgot I was working while stationed there), with all the fun and excitement we had on a daily basis. I also continued to pursue my college education, and while traveling and throughout my career, I knew that nothing was final until the paperwork was done.

After leaving Europe, returning to Fort Rucker was a nice change. I had missed home, and it felt like coming home to very familiar surroundings. I gave birth to my daughter at the post hospital and felt very complete with both of my children with me.

It was a time for family growth; teaching my children how to take the time to smell the flowers was important to me. Together we would pick strawberries, pecans, and even experienced the "picking of cotton" on our weekend outings. It seemed as if Alabama had a pecan tree in every yard.

As a working mother, I felt I had to protect my children in a special way. My mom was always at home for me when I was growing up, and I knew the world had really changed since my upbringing, so I felt living on base would give my children a little more protection and structure. I also enrolled my son in programs to enhance social skills and sport activities, such as soccer. Later I would enroll my son in the Boy Scouts to learn some simple things that our children are forgetting to take a little time to focus on because of television and video games. The scouts helped my son to learn how to become a team player and follow rules, and it helped build his confidence by realizing his ability to meet new challenges and complete small tasks.

I wanted my children to know that there was something bigger than themselves that existed, besides God, and that they must have a respect for authority in and outside of the home. I wanted it to be a permanent part of them like DNA.

My daughter and her first-grade class were interviewed by a local Alabama newspaper. They asked all the children in her class, "What does Thanksgiving mean to you?" My daughter's response was "It means a lot to me. It's part of being good and saying thanks to everybody." When I read the article, I said to myself, "She gets it." And it was gratifying for me because I knew my job was to continue to keep both of my children focused in that direction of thinking in order for them to be successful persons for themselves and our society. That could simply mean opening doors for the elderly or saying "please" and "thank you" when appropriate. I knew that it was essential to begin this training early in a child's life.

Tower buildings in Berlin

SunBeams
By Linda Bryan
SunStylesEditor

What does Thanksg

Parnell Broxton
You can eat turkey, mashed potatoes and homemade biscuits.

Stacey Dugar
It means a lot to me. It's part of being good and saying thanks to everybody.

Casey Hyatt
Nice people to others.

Ben Waldner
I think of my grandparents and my dog that died.

Christi Laird
You give thanks to people that was in the Army and aren't in the Army now.

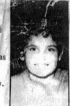

Bubba Se
Going hun for turkeys

Sun Devotional Pa

I sought the Lord, and he answered me; he delivered me from all my fears. Those who look to him are radia never covered with shame.

Courtesy of *SunStyles* editor

Chapter Eighteen

The Storm

I eagerly redeployed back to Germany, a place I learned to love and appreciate. I realized that it is a place we as a country could learn a lot from. Good-quality craftsmanship, especially with their vehicles (I know Chevy has gotten better). Many of their towns are unchanged; they just maintain what they have, and we need to save our trees.

I was stationed in Stuttgart, Germany, and working as an air traffic controller flight operations sergeant. I remember the call from the chain of command. The commander began the first call, and the person he called, in turn, called the next person, and so on down the line; and the word was "Pack your bags, the storm has begun."

My first thought was my children. I had to get them home; even though if you have a family in the military, in cases such as this, there should be someone locally to help supervise or keep your family safe while you deploy or someone can fly in to take control for you.

I was starring in the play *The King and I* with the score of Rodgers and Hammerstein, where we had nightly performances and standing ovations (I had no singing part);

however, upon the beginning of the storm, the play ended as the cast members were slowly being deployed to Saudi Arabia.

I was fortunate that my career field and duty allowed me to stay at Stuttgart Army Airfield and continue to conduct my business as outlined in that war mission by assisting in the deployment of almost all the soldiers in the southern area of Germany to Saudi Arabia. The military airfield and the civilian airport shared the runway in Stuttgart, and the airport was much smaller than Frankfurt's; however, we had a constant flow of 747s and military Galaxy aircraft landing to pick up and drop off soldiers and taxiing to our side of the airfield runway, which was an operation to witness.

I had never felt so much pride in serving in the military at that time, seeing our soldiers—men and women—marching onto those aircraft with their weapons at their sides, into an unknown situation, with their heads held high.

I met General Powell and his wife when they flew into Stuttgart toward the end of the storm, shook his hand, and nodded to his wife as we escorted them off the field and into a waiting vehicle to meet with General Franks, who headed the U.S. Command in Europe with the Desert Storm. My military career culminated as flight operations sergeant and supervisor for instructors, who taught new soldiers coming into the military that job specialty. In addition to my flight operations position, I would narrate post level ceremonies that were held on the post parade field, which included introduction of new military aircraft, change of command, and retirement ceremonies. The one retirement ceremony that stands out in my mind was when the outgoing command sergeant major stood motionless as the bleachers were filled, many as his guests to honor his military service, including service and family members, quite a large crowd of several hundred people; and as I finished speaking the words of his final years of duty, the band picked up the music, and you could feel the distinct sound of the drums rumbling through your body. And as the long line of troop formations passed for review, making every step in perfect unison, I saw the tears begin to flow down his face. He held his position of attention until the end session of soldiers was barely noticeable; the soldiers marched over the small hill on the parade field until they finally went out of sight. With the drum sound still beating through your body, you knew he would remember that moment for the rest of his life.

It was hard to watch the older soldiers cry because they always projected strength when leading; and with their tears coming forth, you know that in their heart they are telling themselves, "I can let go now, a job well done."

CHAPTER NINETEEN

The Apple Does Not Fall Far from the Tree

After my retirement from the military, I became a registered nurse, followed by a physical therapist assistant. While working as a nurse and during many of my visits to patients' homes to provide in-home treatment for them, many conversations with my patients would center on their family. I visited one gentleman in particular (a retired lawyer). When I asked who the people in the picture frames were on his fireplace mantel, he told me they were his son and daughter. He said to me, "My daughter is a judge, and my son is a lawyer." I saw this trend in families I visited more than less, and my family is no different. My son, now a military officer and, might I add, a gentleman, has a military career well toward the direction of retirement; and my daughter also has an air force military career, with her current educational focus on becoming a registered nurse.

CONCLUSION

Timing Is Everything

I remember all my yesterdays as if they just occurred, but how the time has passed so quickly. I've realized that nothing is constant but change, and I feel that with life, you have to be ready to proceed in any direction. Take a chance and make a decision. Whichever direction you choose to take, you must do it to the best of your ability, because people appreciate that; and it can take you far.

I've always said that I would never tell all, but that too has changed, and the time is right now.

IN MY OWN WORDS

RETIRED SFC GLENDA DUGAR

BS in Professional Aeronautics

AS in Applied Science Registered Nursing

AS in Applied Science Physical Therapist Assistant

Iron Mike, 118th MP Company reunion picture, 2013

"In My Own Words"
can be found in the
PRITZKER Military Museum and Library
Chicago, Ill

www. pritzkermilitary.org